IR

TONS of NUMBERS!

by Sarah L. Schuette

A SPOT-IT, LEARN-IT CHALLENGE

A+ books

CAPSTONE PRESS
a capstone imprint

A+ Books are published by Capstone Press,
1710 Roe Crest Drive, North Mankato, Minnesota 56003
www.capstonepub.com

Library of Congress Cataloging-in-Publication Data
Cataloging-in-publication information is on file with the Library of Congress.
ISBN 978-1-4765-5110-4 (board book)
ISBN 978-1-4765-5947-6 (eBook PDF)
ISBN 978-1-4765-4012-2 (library binding)
ISBN 978-1-4765-5102-9 (paperback)

Editorial Credits
Jeni Wittrock, editor; Juliette Peters, designer; Wanda Winch, media researcher;
Eric Manske, production specialist; Sarah Schuette, photo stylist; Marcy Morin,
studio scheduler

The author dedicates this book to her Goddaughter Muriel Hilgers.

Photo Credits
all photos by Capstone Studio/Karon Dubke

Note to Parents, Teachers, and Librarians
Spot It, Learn It! is an interactive series that supports literacy development and
reading enjoyment. Readers utilize visual discrimination skills to find objects among
fun-to-peruse photographs with busy backgrounds. Readers also build vocabulary
through thematic groupings, develop visual memory ability through repeated
readings, and improve strategic and associative thinking skills by experimenting with
different visual search methods.

Printed in the United States of America in Stevens Point, Wisconsin.
092013   00007773WZS14

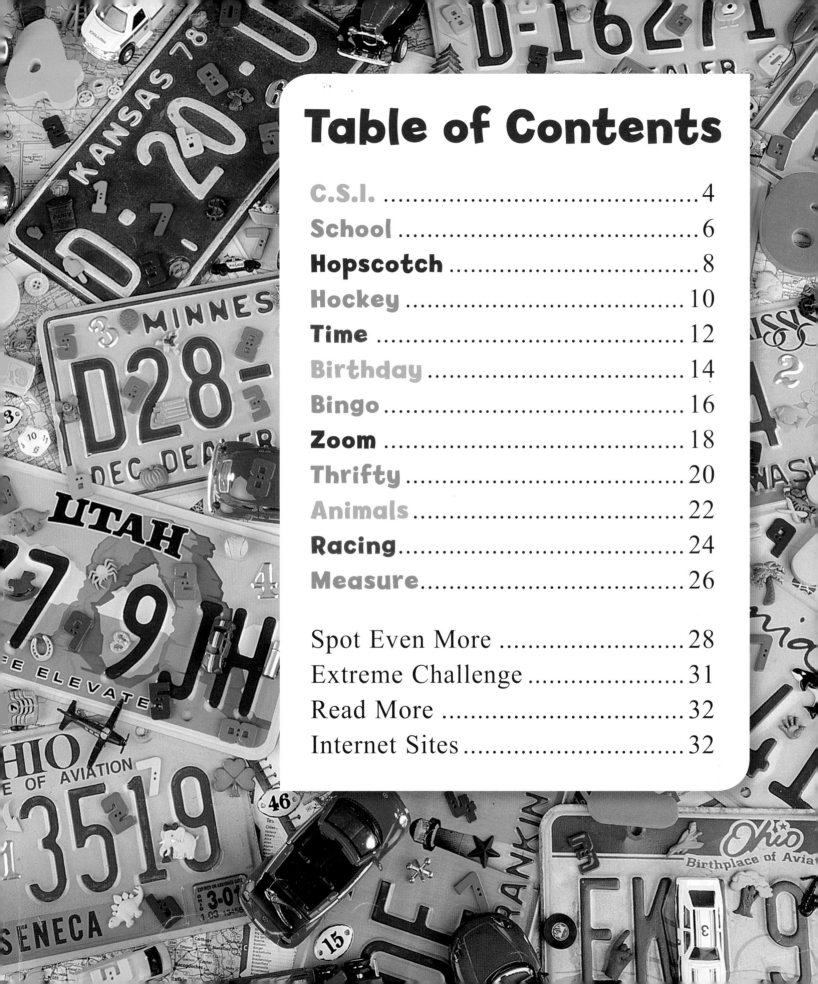

Table of Contents

C.S.I.

Can you find **four 3s**?

Find **one police car**.

Spot a **black 7**.

How many **yellow things** do you see?

How many **black 1s** can you count?

See a **dice rolled to 3**?

Find **one brown peanut**.

CRIME SCEN

EVIDENT
CRIME SCENE PRODUCTS
evidentcrimescene.com
1-800-576-7606

School

Try to spot a **blue 2**.

Next count **3 school buses**.

Find a **black 2**.

Count all of the **forks**.

What number is on the **milk carton**?

How many **bag lunches** do you see?

Count the **airplanes**.

Hopscotch

Find **three basketballs**.

Spot **five baseballs**.

Count all of the **green chalk pieces**.

Find a **black dice rolled to 3**.

How many **footballs** can you count?

Spot a **blue 33**.

Count the **chalk stars**.

Hockey

Look for a **blue 4**.

Count all of the **pink numbers**.

Add a **yellow 8** and **yellow 2** together.

Spot a **black 6**.

How many **skates** do you see?

What number is on the **black shirt**?

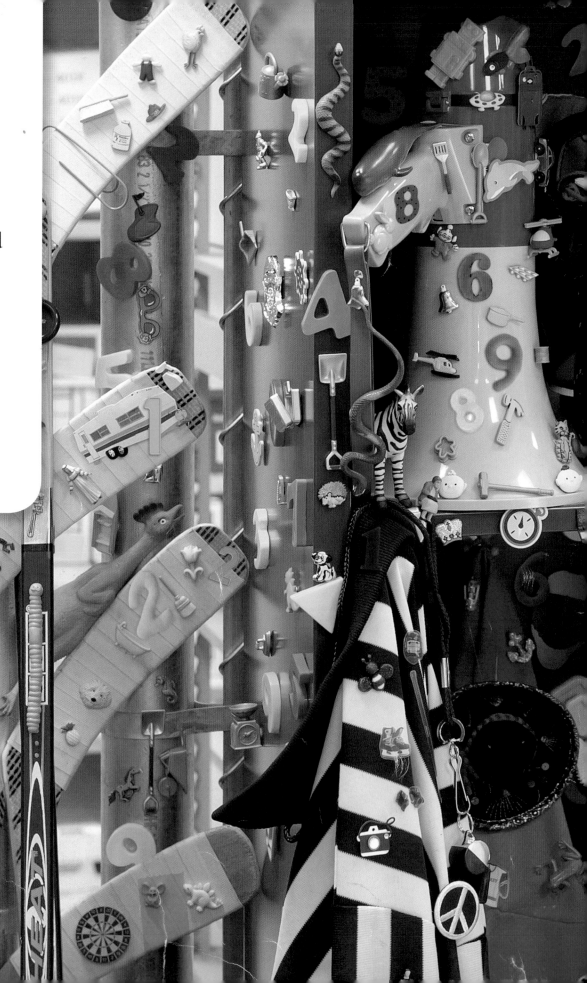

Time

How many **clocks** do you see?

Where is a **red 18**?

Find **one pink heart**.

Next find two **red 5s**.

What number are the **green pliers** pointing to?

Find the **white 35**.

Spot **two flamingos**.

12

Birthday

Find **three soccer balls**.

How many **holes** are in each **button**?

How many **stripes** are on the **bowling pins**?

Can you spot **two cupcakes**?

What number is the **bone** on?

Find **six purple things**.

Bingo

Try to find all of the **7s**.

Count the **yellow stars**.

Can you see **two dinosaurs**?

Where's the **red 52**?

Spot **two sheep**.

How many **white dice** do you see?

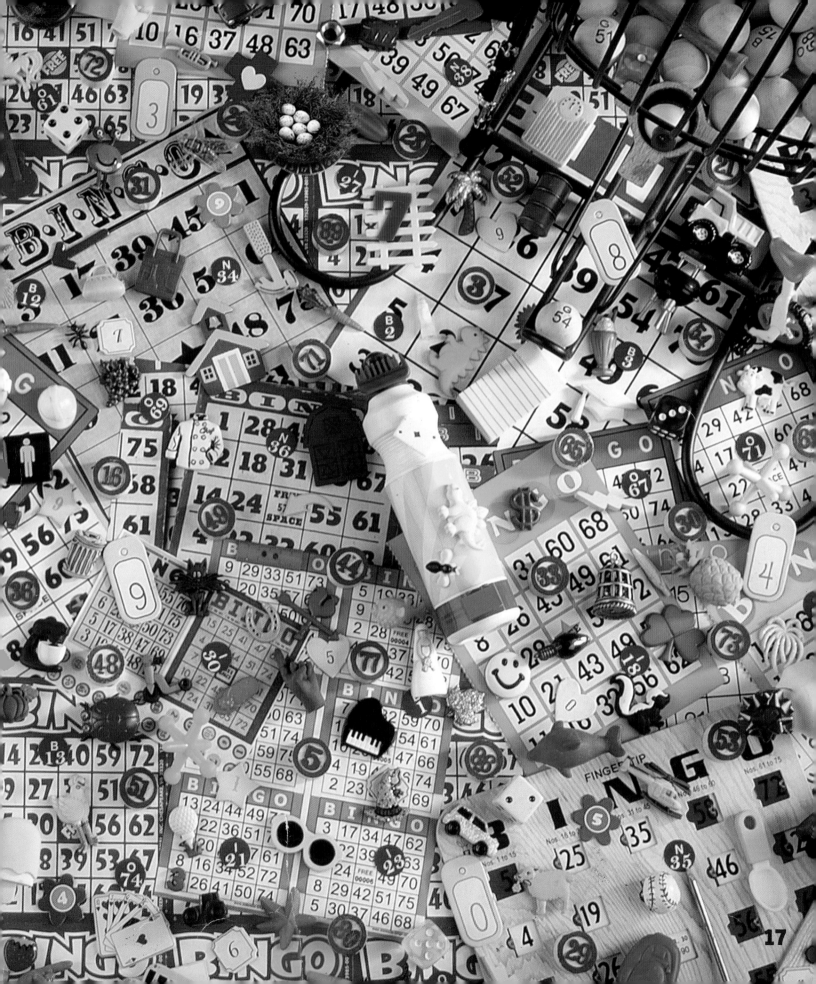

Zoom

Count the **license plates**.

Find a **blue 8**.

Spot an **orange 8**.

Count all of the **yellow numbers**.

See if you can find a car with a **green 5**.

Look for a **silver 9**.

How many numbers are on the **Kansas license plate**?

Thrifty

Search for a **blue 9**.

Find a jersey with an **orange 9**.

Count **nine price tags**.

Find a **white 3**.

Find **two gnomes**.

How much does the **red pepper** cost?

Count all of the **pieces of fruit**.

40% OFF

35% OFF

$2

$1

SALE PRICE

$1

$1

7

$3

75¢

$1

25¢

45¢

75¢

99¢

1

25% OFF

SALE

EVERY WEDNESDAY
4:00pm – 8:00pm
● 20 % OFF
● 50 % OFF
● 70 % OFF

50¢

50¢

75¢

$2

$2

LAND O LAKES

75¢

75¢

25¢

SALE PRICE

25

$1

$1

$1

9

$1

50¢

50¢

$1

50¢

50¢

5 1

SALE NOW ON

WILL RETURN

3

7

4

50¢

SALE PRICE

$2

30% OFF
sale · sale · sale

6

9

$1

5

8

New 2 You Treasures

$3

60¢

21

Animals

Can you count **ten animals**?

Find **one raccoon**.

Do you see the word **three**?

Spot **one hamburger**.

Count the **acorns** that you find.

Find a **black 18**.

How many **rungs** are on the **brown ladder**?

Racing

Spot **two yellow 5**s.

Find a **blue 15**.

Count the **red cars**.

Spot a **gold 45**.

Can you see a **green 3**?

Where is a **dragon with 2 heads**?

Find **one hotdog**.

Measure

Look for a **black 50**.

Where's **one strawberry**?

Find a **star button with 5 holes.**

Spot a **dime**. How much is it worth?

How many **orange things** can you count?

Count the **leaves on the green shamrock**.

How many **9s** can you find?

Spot Even More

Bingo • page 16

How many spots are on the **red 7**? Look for an **orange 0**. Count the **eggs** in the **nest**. Now find a **white 18**.

Zoom • page 18

Spot a **purple 1**. Can you count all of the **spiders**? Find the **red 7**. Spot all of the **green cars**.

Thrifty • page 20

How much do the **blue drinking glasses** cost? Find a **yellow 5**. Count **two red game pieces**. Do you see **two pieces of bread**?

Animals • page 22

Spot all of the **brown rabbits**. How many **houses** do you see? Find a **brown 4**. How many **tusks** does the **mastodon** have?

Racing • page 24

How many **green cars** do you see? Spot the **black 9**. Find **five white dots on a dice**.

Measure • page 26

Spot two **letter J**s. Find a **red 30**. Where's the **orange 80**? How many **dots** are on the **pink and green party hat**?

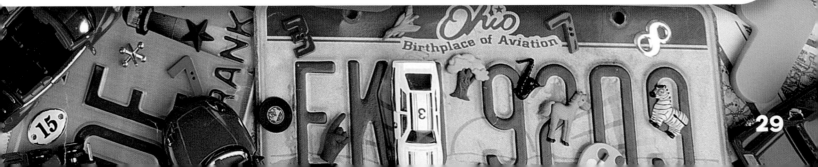

Extreme Challenge

Just can't get enough Spot-It action? Here's an extra numbers challenge.

Where's a **gingerbread man with two buttons**?

Find a **blue 4**.

Count all of the **brown things**.

Now find **one hotdog**.

How many **buttons are on the pink cell phone**?

Spot an **orange dice with 3 dots**.

Now find **4 shoes**.

Look for the all of the **0s.**

Where are **2 lizards**?

Count the **spots on the ladybug**.

Which **tractor** has **7** below it?

Count the **horseshoe's spots**.

What **numbers** are on the **screen of the red calculator**?

Read More

Ghigna, Charles. *Numbers at the Park: 1-10.* Learning Parade. North Mankato, Minn.: Picture Window Books, 2013.

Menotti, Andrea. *How Many Jelly Beans?* San Francisco: Chronicle Books, 2012.

Schuette, Sarah L. *Science Fun: A Spot-It Challenge.* Spot It. North Mankato, Minn.: Capstone Press, 2012.

Internet Sites

FactHound offers a safe, fun way to find Internet sites related to this book. All of the sites on FactHound have been researched by our staff.

Here's all you do:

Visit *www.facthound.com*

Type in this code: 9781476540122

Super-cool stuff! Check out projects, games and lots more at **www.capstonekids.com**